Tigers

Meredith Hooper

These are Sumatran
tiger cubs.

Oxford

Oxford University Press, Great Clarendon Street, Oxford, OX2 6DP

Oxford New York
Athens Auckland Bangkok Bogota Buenos Aires
Calcutta Cape Town Chennai Dar es Salaam Delhi
Florence Hong Kong Istanbul Karachi Kuala Lumpur
Madrid Melbourne Mexico City Mumbai Nairobi Paris
São Paulo Singapore Taipei Tokyo Toronto Warsaw

and associated companies in
Berlin Ibadan

Oxford is a trade mark of Oxford University Press

Text © Meredith Hooper 1999
First published by Oxford University Press 1999
All rights reserved
A CIP record for this book is available from the British Library

ISBN 0 19 915561 5
Available in packs
Animals Pack of Six   (one of each book)   ISBN 0 19 915567 4
Animals Class Pack   (six of each book)   ISBN 0 19 915618 2

Acknowledgements

The Publisher would like to thank the following for permission to reproduce photographs:

The Bridgeman Art Library: pp 7, 8/9;   The British Museum: pp 5 (P5290894), 11 (*bottom*) (P5202834);   Britstock-IFA/Amadeus: p 4 (*bottom left*); Britstock-IFA/Schmidbauer: p 13 (*top*);   Bruce Coleman/Alain Compost: p 6 (*bottom*);   Bruce Coleman/Gunter Ziesler: p 3;   Bruce Coleman/Jean-Pierre Zwaenepoel: pp 6 (*middle*), 10 (*middle*);   Kodansha Ltd, Tokyo/Tenkyu-in Temple in Myoshin-ji: p 12;   Oxford Scientific Films/Bob Bennett: p 6 (*top*); Oxford Scientific Films/Mahipal Singh: p 13 (*bottom*);   Oxford Scientific Films/ Belinda Wright: p 11(*top*);   Planet Earth Pictures: p 4 (*bottom right*);   Planet Earth Pictures/Thomas Dressler: p 4 (*top left*);   Planet Earth Pictures/ Jonathon Scott: p 4 (*top right*);   Planet Earth Pictures/Anup Shah: p 10 (*top*); Tony Stone Images/Schafer & Hill: Titlepage and back cover;   Tony Stone Images/Manoj Shah: p 10 (*bottom*).

With thanks to London Zoo, Conservation in Action and The Environmental Investigation Agency (EIA) for the use of material.

Front cover photograph is by Corel.

The paintings: p 5 Tiger, After Chen Zuzhong, early thirteenth century;
p 7 detail from Yoko and the Tiger from 24 Paragons of Filial Piety;
p 9 Tropical Storm with a Tiger by Henri Rousseau, nineteenth century;
p 11 Tiger, Kishi Ganku, eighteenth century;
p 12 Tigers in a bamboo grove, Sanraku and Sahsetsu, seventeenth century;
p 15 Tiger in the Stream by Lulu Wong Taylor, twentieth century.

Printed in Hong Kong

Contents

Tigers' paw prints are called "pug marks".

What is a tiger?

Tigers are cats. Lions, leopards, and pet cats are all cats as well.

lion

leopard

pet cat

tiger

But tigers are the biggest cats in the world.

Paintings of tigers

People like painting pictures of tigers.
This painting shows how big and
powerful tigers are.

This
picture
was
painted
in China.

Where tigers live

All wild tigers live in Asia.

Bengal tiger
Some tigers live in warm,
dry forests.

Siberian tiger
Some tigers live in
cold, snowy woods.

**Sumatran
tiger**
Some tigers
live in hot,
steamy
jungles.

Tigers live alone. Each tiger needs its own territory where it can find water and food.

This picture was painted in Japan. ▼

Tiger stripes

A tiger has between 100 and 150 stripes on its fur. Each tiger has a different pattern of stripes.

Henri Rousseau

Stripes help tigers to hide. Stripes help tigers to look like their surroundings. This is called "camouflage".

This picture was painted in France. The stripes camouflage the tiger.

Tigers are hunters

Tigers eat animals like deer, wild pigs, and wild cattle. The animals that tigers hunt are called their "prey".

A tiger creeps up on its prey.

Then it pounces.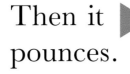

The tiger eats as much as it can. Then it rests.

When the tiger is hungry it hunts again.

This picture of a tiger hunting was painted in Japan.

Tiger cubs

Tiger cubs drink milk from their mother. They begin to eat meat when they are about two months old.

This picture of a tiger and her cub was painted in Japan.

The mother tiger
looks after her
cubs until
they are two
or three
years old.

Then the cubs
leave their
mother to live
alone.

Tigers in danger

Wild tigers are in great danger.

Some people cut down
the forests where tigers live. Some
people kill tigers. There are not many
wild tigers left.

Some people are trying to save wild tigers. If wild tigers are not saved, there will only be photographs and paintings left.

 This picture of a wild tiger was painted in the UK in 1996.

a b c d e f g h i j k l m n o p q r s t u v w x y z

Sources

The author got information for this book from the World Wide Fund for Nature, Global Tiger Patrol, the Cat Specialist Group of the World Conservation Union, Survival Special (Anglia TV), and The International Tiger Information Center on the Internet.

Index